CHRISTIANITY AND DEMOCRACY

CHRISTIANITY
and
DEMOCRACY

BY

Jacques Maritain

Translated by
DORIS C. ANSON

New York
CHARLES SCRIBNER'S SONS
1944

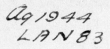

IN
HOMAGE
TO
THE
PEOPLE OF FRANCE

CONTENTS

PREFACE

THIS LITTLE BOOK was written during the summer of 1942, at a time when the outcome of the war could still seem very disquieting. It appeared in French early in the Spring of 1943, at a time when, whatever acts of desperation or machiavellianism Germany might yet try, her defeat and that of her partners seemed certain. The certitude of the Allied victory is even greater at the moment of writing.

At this stage of a military war which is also a general liquidation and revolution it so happens that, as the hope of winning the war becomes more firmly fixed in our hearts, anxiety increases as to whether the peace will be won. Some of us, even without sharing Pearl Buck's pessimism, wonder sometimes whether we have not expected too much of a war of liberation, and shall not have to say with Isaiah: *Behold, in peace is my bitterest bitterness*. As a matter of fact it would have been naïve to believe that the liberation of the world

would be the immediate fruit of victory. War
was unleashed because the world was too sick
and this kind of sickness is not cured at one stroke.
What we could have hoped, what we can and
must still hope, is that victory, by destroying the
totalitarian enslaver's fury, will not only unlock
the gates of history and open the way to constructive work, but will truly establish the definite
conditions previously required by this work. Moreover, if the struggle of those who are fighting
Nazism and its satellites is not truly animated by
an heroic ideal of the liberation of human life, and
if victory is not to bring about the foundations of
a world reorganization which enlists men's efforts
in a common task dominated by such an ideal,
civilization will have escaped from the imminent
threat of destruction only to embark on a period of
chaos, when, after having militarily wiped out
Fascism and Nazism, it will run the risk of being
morally conquered by their substitutes.

The truth is that war in itself has no transforming power. In itself it blows up the mecha-
nisms and surface forces which sustained, after a
fashion, a disintegrating order; but in itself it
gives free rein, not to the new, but to the accumu-

lated though not manifested forces *already existing*—latent forces more or less driven back and repressed, but already formed, already prepared. That is why the work of recovery and purification which was under way before the war becomes more urgent than ever during the war. It must be speeded up during the war as much as the war industries and the technical inventions. It is from this work that we may expect a transforming power. The creation of a new world will not be the work of the war, but of the force of vision and will, and of the energies of intellectual and moral reform which will have developed in the collective conscience and in the responsible leaders—if these forces become sufficiently strong and succeed in triumphing over adverse potentialities which are also present in history and which, in their turn, exert pressure to become realities.

It is therefore not surprising that in the tremendous surge of events in which the war sweeps us along—more changeable than the sea or the storm—an obscure and hidden struggle between the historical currents and forces which contend for the mind and heart of men is taking place at the same moment as the visible ups and downs of the military conflict. In the latter as in the former, all the threats do not materialize, and what seems at one moment an imminent danger can fade the following moment, and give way to another peril or to a fortunate conjuncture. Old pre-war dangers—sometimes class-selfishness, sometimes the maneuvers and foolish fancies of certain possessing groups, and those reflexes of blind collective fear which, instead of ridding Communism of its pretexts, run the risk of casting part of the world to Communism, or of bringing on civil war on the morrow of peace; sometimes the fondness, in those who have forgotten nothing and have learned nothing for the false philosophy of life, for the old forms of anarchic individualism and for the bigoted dread of the Gospel which have spiritually disarmed the democracies and ruined from within their authentic vital principle; sometimes the illusion, springing up here and there, which seeks to make of the power of a German national state and of the German army a bulwark against Russia, without seeing the danger of revolutionary alliances or the danger of a new war which may thus be prepared, and without realizing that the only chance of avoiding the perils which the democracies fear is by attempting to reinstate the Russian people in the western community; sometimes the old dream of the restoration of the dynasties in Europe and of a union of authoritative "Latin" states, and sometimes the possibility of a return, after victory, to the policy of two fronts, "popular front" and "reactionary front" which brought about the misfortune of the European nations and which sapped their vital energies—old pre-war dangers suddenly cause frightful possibilities to emerge on the surface of the water. It is up to the effort of men of courage, faith and informed reason to keep these possibilities from becoming other than historical potentialities. Truth to tell, many of these objects of fear are already ghosts, and what frightens us is occasionally nothing but the dead burying their dead. Today history is moving like an avalanche toward good and toward evil. The good or evil occurrences which will appear before our eyes will doubtless exceed our forecast and imagination.

In such conjunctures, hope is not only more reasonable than any definite prejudice of optimism or pessimism, it is also a force and a spiritual weapon, as necessary a dynamic agent of effective transformation and victory as material weapons and munitions. It is an historic duty, a duty to our brothers and to future generations to keep hope firm, and not to waver at the sight of the clouds which form and fade on the horizon. The obscure hope of millions of men is at work in the underground recesses of history. We must hope with them that the peace will be won, and act in pursuance of that hope. We must hope with them that victory will open up an era of constructive work dedicated to the true enfranchisement of human life. We must hope with them that in spite of the too-real difficulties amongst which human prudence flounders, those who lead the peoples will take the risk of putting their trust in the peoples, I meant first and foremost in those peoples already acclimated to liberty; and that in spite of the fevers to which the diverse nations will be exposed, either as a result of the long and unutterable tortures they have undergone, or as a result of final victory itself, the spirit of national claims and national pride will give way to the spirit of a supra-national community; and we must hope with them that in spite of the physical and moral exhaustion of the peoples, the vital energies hidden in them, and first and foremost in those peoples acclimated to liberty, will rouse the men needed and open up the path to a new civilization and a new democracy whose Christian inspiration will call forth not only, in the West, the living traditions of Christ's religion, but, throughout the world, the moral forces of "the naturally Christian soul."

This little book will perhaps seem too optimistic to readers of quick judgment. Optimism had no part in its inspiration. It did not spring from an optimistic state of mind; it sprang from hope and from a deliberate will to hope. Its purpose is to indicate the direction in which I believe we will have to proceed, not to mark the stages or guess at the time it will take to overcome the obstacles met along the way. The immediate future is of terrible moment to us, to us and to all that we hold dear. Yet once it has been freed from the perils of total and irremediable destruction like those which it combats today, human civilization will have time. If it is a question of the full realization of the historical ideal for which we hope, it is to be reached, we believe, only at the time which the apostle Paul heralds as the richness of the world and a resurrection from the dead. But in the meantime we must act and fight, and advance in the right direction; the creative forces must be set going again, and the movement of the temporal community must find once again its normal line of development.

J. M.

New York,
October 2, 1943

THE END OF AN AGE

IF WE WANT to take the measure of the horrible war that the Pagan Empire has unleashed on the peoples of the earth and which kills not only men but consciences as well, wears nations threadbare, starves the children and destroys throughout Europe and the world the vital resources of the generations to come, we must understand that it is a moment of paroxysm in the liquidation of a world. The end of the Roman Empire was a minor event compared with what we behold. We are looking on at the liquidation of what is known as the "modern world" which ceased to be modern a quarter of a century ago when the First World War marked its entry into the past. The question is: in what will this liquidation result? The answer depends primarily upon the force of arms. If the Axis powers win the war, night will settle down on the world and freedom will die for centuries to come—all the freedoms, and honor, and the very possibility of living as a man. If the United

Nations win the war, the way is opened to constructive work. But the answer does not depend alone on the force of arms. The war will not be truly won, the peace will not be won, unless during the war itself a new world takes shape which will emerge in victory—and in which the classes, races and nations today oppressed will be liberated. The war will not be truly won, the peace will not be won, unless the people *understand* and unless the intellectual and moral reform effected within them is equal to the suffering of their present martyrdom, and equal to the breadth of social transformations alike necessary if civilization is to survive. The anguish of mankind demands not merely to know whether the free peoples will have enough munitions, enough soldiers. It also demands to know whether the free peoples will understand the meaning of the trial in which they are engaged, whether their will and intelligence will be a match for the historical event, whether they will purify their actions and their thoughts, their philosophy of life and their political philosophy. With the nations of Europe plunged in the abyss of distress, we know at all events that the work of redress and purification is taking place in them silently—wherever an heroic faith says *no* to the oppressor and his henchmen. The awareness that the American people are achieving of their responsibilities, the flame of idealism with which their soldiers face death, prove that this work is also taking place in them with the obscure force of profound germination. It will have to take place in all the corners of the earth where man accepts sacrifice and death for the sake of liberty.

Cast into the same furnace, threatened in the same elementary rights, resisting evil destiny with the same hope and the same anger, all the peoples who have decided to put an end to the enslaver's barbarism will have to choose, after victory, and are already having to choose during the war, between a common task of heroic renewal and the old selfishness and the old covetousness which would start up chaos all over again. America and the United Nations will win the war. But enslaved Europe will win it with them, and the hell through which she has passed will have given her terrible rights over the future, either to perpetuate the tempest if she is driven to despair, or to play her part in the advent of a better and more human common life.

I have spoken of a work of purification; this expression is accurate in itself, yet I use it with slight misgivings and I should not like to have it misinterpreted.

Men contaminated by Fascism and Nazism do much more than lie: they have perverted the function of language. In France the Pétain régime has sought to spread through the nation a pharisaical ideology, wherein all these venerable words like penitence, compunction, purification of the heart and of customs, have lost their sense and their honor, and become synonyms of sickly self-accusation which is demanded of enslaved people in order to furnish the really guilty ones with an alibi. The work of purification today demanded of men is not an escape into the commonplaces of a morality which has been turned into a shelter for political resentments and class hatreds, and into a glorification of the whip. It is not an epidemic of senile resignation. It is a work of courage and hope, of confidence and faith, which must begin with an effort of the mind determined to see clearly at all cost, and to rescue from the errors which disfigured them the great things in which we have believed and in which we believe, and which are the hope of the world.

We are looking on at the liquidation of the modern world—of that world which was led by Machiavelli's pessimism to regard unjust force as the essence of politics; which Luther's scission unbalanced, by withdrawing Germany from the European community; wherein the absolutism of the Ancient Régime changed the Christian order by degrees into an order of compulsion ever more separated from the Christian roots of life; which the rationalism of Descartes and the Encyclopedists swept into an illusory optimism; which the pseudo-Christian naturalism of Jean-Jacques Rousseau led to confound the sacred aspirations of the heart of man with the expectation of a kingdom of God on earth procured by the State or by the Revolution; which Hegel's pantheism taught to deify its own historical movement; and whose decline was precipitated by the advent of the bourgeois class, the capitalist profit system, the imperialistic conflicts and unbridled absolutism of the national States. This world was born of Christendom and owed its deepest living strength to the Christian tradition. It was all the more severely judged for this. Its ultimate error lay in believing that man is saved by his own strength alone, and that human history is made without God. But this world has been great and has done great works; man has taken on a more profound awareness of himself and of his dignity, and of the law which calls him to advance in time; civil society on the one hand, rational knowledge on the other, have here achieved their autonomy. Science and the scientific conquest of nature, industry and technology, have known wondrous successes—while taking, to our misfortune, the place of wisdom; the machine has brought unheard-of possibilities of emancipation against the day when human reason will have learned how to regulate its use for truly human ends. Ever since the French Revolution and the effusion of secularized Christian idealism which it provoked in history, the sense of freedom and the sense of social justice have convulsed and vitalized our civilization; and one would need to have the soul of a slave to wish for the destruction of this very sense of freedom and justice on account of the suffering and disorder it may have occasioned. In short, at the same time that there fructified in the modern world the evils whose seed this world bore within itself, the natural growth of civilization and the inner work due to the evangelical ferment continued within it. Nineteenth century civilization did not know how to manage, but it nonetheless preserved in its foundations the heritage of divine and human values which emanates from our fathers' struggle for freedom, from the Judeo-Christian tradition and from classical antiquity. And it remained, for all that, Christian in the actual principles to which it owed its existence, even though it misjudged them abundantly—in the sacred roots to which still clung its idea of man and human progress, of law and the value of the spirit—in the religious liberty which it willy-nilly preserved, however opposed it may have been at certain moments and in certain countries—and even in the very trust in reason and in man's greatness which its free-thinkers fashioned into a weapon against Christianity—and in the secularized Christian feeling which despite erroneous ideologies inspired its political and social achievements and expectations.

If the ever-growing schism between the true behavior of our world and the moral and spiritual principles on which its firmness depended, were to bring about a fatal rupture in balance, if our world has little by little been emptied of its spirit, and has seemed at length a universe of words, an unleavened mass, if the catastrophe has become inevitable, the tremendous historical fund of energy and truth accumulated for centuries is still available to human freedom, the forces of renewal are on the alert and it is still up to us to make sure that this catastrophe of the modern world is not a regression to a perverted aping of the Ancient Régime or of the Middle Ages, and that it does not wind up in the totalitarian putrefaction of the German New Order. It is up to us rather to see that it emerges in a new and truly creative age, where man, in suffering and hope, will resume his journey toward the conquest of freedom.

THE TRAGEDY OF THE DEMOCRACIES

THE TRAGEDY OF THE modern democracies is that they have not yet succeeded in realizing democracy. The causes of this failure are many. First, the enemies of the democratic ideal never laid down their arms; and their resentment, their hatred of the people, and of freedom, have only grown in proportion as the weaknesses and errors of the modern democracies gave them more pretexts. Finally a coalition was effected between the interests of the ruling classes, corrupted by money, desperately clinging to their privileges and crazed by a blind fear of Communism (the spread of which could have been prevented only by a clear-sighted policy of social reform), and the ambitions of sordid adventurers and the slave philosophy taught in all the countries of Europe by utopians, eager to see their ideas prevail through any means whatsoever, by sadistic racists, drunk with the joy of using the spirit to betray the spirit, and by vulgar traffickers in human degradation. At the very moment when all the stratagems of intellectual intimidation, pseudo-scientific or pseudo-literary prestige and calumny were carrying this sham ideology to its greatest efficacy, the youth of the democratic countries was giving itself up to a soul-searching from which it would have emerged a few years later with renewed strength. But the first effect of this self-examination was to develop doubt and hesitancy, and the youth was to conclude it in prisons and concentration camps, and by offering heroic resistance to the Beast that is trampling Europe under foot.

Another great reason for the failure of the modern democracies to realize democracy is the fact that this realization inevitably demanded accomplishment in the social as well as in the political order, and that this demand was not complied with. The irreducible antagonisms inherent in an economy based on the self-propagating power of money, the selfishness of the monied classes, and the secession of the proletariat raised by Marxism to the mystic principle of the Revolution, all prevented the democratic tenets from being incorporated into social life; and the impotence of modern societies in the face of poverty and the dehumanization of work, coupled with their inability to transcend the exploitation of man by man, have been a bitter failure for them.

But the principal reason is of a spiritual nature. It lies in the inner contradiction and the tragic misunderstanding of which the modern democracies, particularly in Europe, have been the victims. This form and this ideal of common life, which we call democracy, springs in its essentials from the inspiration of the Gospel and cannot subsist without it; and by virtue of the blind logic of historical conflicts and habits of social memory, which has nothing whatever to do with the logic of thought, we saw for a century the motivating forces in the modern democracies repudiating the Gospel and Christianity in the name of human liberty, while motivating forces in the Christian social strata were combating the democratic aspirations in the name of religion. In France the labor movement of 1848 was animated by a Christian flame, however smoky this flame may at times have been. The free-thinking bourgeoisie smothered both the movement and the flame; and at that moment the social power of religion worked for the bourgeoisie as it had worked in the past for the policy of "the throne and the altar." The licensed apostles of social emancipation were no longer able to recognize Jesus in the Church and mistook religious orthodoxy for the political and social oppression which set itself up as the upholder of order. The social supporters of religion were no longer able to recognize Jesus in the poor and in the confused outcry of their demands, and mistook every call to social justice for the upheaval and the Godless Revolution which proclaimed itself progress. The great scandal of which Pius XI spoke * seemed consummated at the end of the nineteenth century. The working classes sought their salvation in the denial of Christianity; the conservative Christian circles sought theirs in the denial of the temporal exigencies of justice and love. The Catholic Church had solemnly warned the peoples against the evil at work in them. These great warnings came too late. Soon panic-stricken guides were pretending to force men to

---

* "The great scandal of the nineteenth century is that the Church lost the working class." Quoted by Abbé Cardijn, founder of the J.O.C. (Catholic Working Youth), after an interview with Pope Pius XI.

choose between Communism, which sought to expel God, and Fascism, which sought to enslave and regiment Him, to corrupt religion in the souls and "dechristianize the Church herself." And this absurd dilemma was to reveal the frightful paralysis to which the inner contradiction just mentioned was to lead both the democratic principle and the Christian principle in the temporal life of the peoples, and was to reveal the calamity produced in the modern democracies by the divorce between these two principles. Men were tragically awakened by the war. If the democracies are to win the peace after having won the war, it will be on condition that the Christian inspiration and the democratic inspiration recognize each other and become reconciled.

There is in America a dangerous plant known as poison ivy. When poison ivy climbs about an oak tree, the oak in its turn becomes dangerous to the touch, and it is called—wrongly so—"poison oak"; the tree is healthy and its sap is healthy; it is the parasite that is poisonous. For thirty years in Europe many sincere minds—not to mention the purveyors of dictatorship and those who cried, "death to the intellect!" turned away from democracy with more or less distaste, so badly was its genuine principle smothered by the poison ivy * which preyed upon it as a parasite. They realize now that in laying the axe to the tree it was the temporal hope of humanity that men were striking without reaching the death elements wound about it. By falling to the ground and living on all the putrefaction of the earth, the poison plants multiplied all the more horribly, producing an evil growth which had the appearance of a fruit. All their poisons were concentrated in the Hitlerian monstrosity.

We do not change at will the names for which generations of men have suffered and hoped. It is not a question of finding a new name for democracy, but rather of discovering its true essence and of realizing it; it is rather a question of passing from bourgeois democracy, drawn dry by its

* This story about poison oak and poison ivy was told me by an American friend with great decisiveness and unquestionable certainty. I believed it. According to information from competent botanists, it appears to be a popular legend. Poison oak and poison ivy are but one and the same *Rhus toxicodendron*. I make atonement to Botanical Science. Yet, following the example of St. Francis of Sales, I think it is permissible to be free in the use of metaphors, and to make use of questionable stories as images destined to illustrate some truth.

hypocrisies and by a lack of evangelical sap, to an integrally human democracy; from abortive democracy to real democracy.

The very name democracy has a different ring in America and in Europe (without entering here into a discussion of the differences existing in this regard between the countries of Europe). In America, where, despite the influence wielded by the great economic interests, democracy has penetrated more profoundly into existence, and where it has never lost sight of its Christian origin, this name conjures up a living instinct stronger than the errors of the spirit which prey upon it. In Europe it conjures up an ideal scoffed at by reality, and whose soul has been half devoured by these same errors.

Perhaps it is because in America Christianity has taken on diffuse and diluted shapes, often to the point of being nothing more than a sentimental ingredient of human morality, that the divorce between the democratic principle and the Christian principle has never made itself as intensely felt here as in Europe, where minds are divided between a Christianity which is irreducibly formed in its structure and its doctrine, but which has been separated for too many years from the life of the people, and open and militant infidelity or hatred of religion. America's problem is to place its Christianity once again within the reach of divine exigency, and to raise up the religious and spiritual potential of its democracy to the height of the cross. Europe's problem is to recover the vivifying power of Christianity in temporal existence, and to put an end at one stroke to the wave of anti-Christian barbarism and the wave of anti-democratic enslavement. Here and there a radical change is needed, a resurrection of the spiritual forces, a new knighthood emanating from the peoples. The change is beginning, it is only just beginning.

THREE REMARKS

IN ORDER TO AVOID misunderstandings, I should like to make three remarks. First, the word democracy, as used by modern peoples, has a wider meaning than in the classical treatises on the science of government. It designates first and foremost a general philosophy of human and political life, and a state of mind. This philosophy and this state of mind do not exclude *a priori* any of the "régimes" or "forms of government" which were recognized as legitimate by classical tradition, that is, recognized as compatible with human dignity. Thus a monarchic régime can be democratic, if it is consistent with this state of mind and with the principles of this philosophy. However, from the moment that historical circumstances lend themselves, the dynamism of democratic thought leads, as though to its most natural form of realization, to the system of government of the same name, which consists, in the words of Abraham Lincoln, in "government of the people, by the people, for the people."

Secondly—and with regard to the present state of the world—it is obvious that after victory the liberated peoples should be allowed to procure for themselves the régime of their choice, or—if they already had such a régime, as the republican régime in the case of the French people—the new constitution of their choice: that is in itself an axiom of democratic thought. But it is no less obvious that no lasting peace will be possible if the régimes in question do not imply approval of the essential bases of common life, respect for human dignity and the rights of the person. Indeed, we may be quite sure that as a very consequence of the torture and oppression which the Pagan Empire has imposed upon men, it is toward the ideal of liberty, equality, fraternity—or, according to the American motto, freedom, justice and happiness— that they will passionately turn, even in those countries which did not have the democratic tradition. Nevertheless the danger of new forms of dictatorship, arising out of wretchedness and resentment, or out of nationalistic impulses, and the danger caused by the mental habits of those peoples not accustomed to freedom who hereditarily worship military force and whose youth has been poisoned by Nazi nihilism, these dangers will be overcome only by great political vigilance, and by a long process of education, which will require the free peoples to look after their brothers with as much justice and charity as firmness. We must understand that the meaning of the present war is not only to put an end to Fascism, Racism, and Militarism, but decidedly to undertake the slow and difficult construction of a world where fear and wretchedness will no longer press down upon individuals and nations; where blindly demanding nationalisms will give way to an organized international community; where the oppression and exploitation of man by man will be abolished; and where everyone will be able to share in the common heritage of civilization and to live a truly human life. In heretofore unseen proportions, from the point of view of its world-wide extension as well as of the depth of the changes which it proclaims, the present war is and must be a war of liberation. The blood of so many men is not being shed in order to impose the democratic form of government upon all peoples; it is being shed so that there may in all prevail that consciousness of the mission of our kind to bring about in its temporal life the law of brotherly love and the spiritual dignity of the human person, which consciousness is the soul of democracy.

In the third place—with regard to the relationship between politics and religion—it is obvious that Christianity and Christian faith can neither be made subservient to democracy as a philosophy of human and political life nor to any political form whatsoever. That is a result of the fundamental distinction introduced by Christ between the things that are Caesar's and the things that are God's, a distinction which has been unfolding throughout our history in the midst of accidents of all kinds, and which frees religion from all temporal enslavement by stripping the State of all sacred pretensions; in other words, by giving the State secular standing. No doctrine or opinion of merely human origin, no matter how true it may be, but only things revealed by God, force themselves upon the faith of the Christian soul. One can be a Christian and achieve one's salvation while militating in favor of any political régime whatsoever, always on condition that it does not trespass against natural law and the law of God. One can be a Christian and achieve one's salvation while defending a political philosophy other than the democratic philosophy, just as one was able to be a Christian, in the days of the Roman Empire, while accepting the social régime of slavery, or in the seventeenth century while holding to the political régime of the absolute monarchy.

But the important thing for the political life of the world and for the solution of the crisis of civilization is by no means to pretend that Christianity is linked to democracy and that Christian faith compels every believer to be a democrat; it is to affirm that democracy is linked to Christianity and that the democratic impulse has arisen in human history as a temporal manifestation of the inspiration of the Gospel. The question does not deal here with Christianity as a religious creed and road to eternal life, but rather with Christianity as leaven in the social and political life of nations and as bearer of the temporal hope of mankind; it does not deal with Christianity as a treasure of divine truth sustained and propagated by the Church, but with Christianity as historical energy at work in the world. It is not in the heights of theology, it is in the depths of the secular conscience and secular existence that Christianity works in this fashion, while sometimes even assuming heretical forms or forms of revolt where it seems to be denying itself, as though the broken bits of the key to paradise, falling into our destitute lives and combining with the metals of the earth, were more effective in activating the history of this world than the pure essence of the celestial metal. It was not given to believers faithful to Catholic dogma but to rationalists to proclaim in France the rights of man and of the citizen, to Puritans to strike the last blow at slavery in America, to atheistic Communists to abolish in Russia the absolutism of private profit. This last process would have been less vitiated by the force of error and would have occasioned fewer catastrophes, had it been performed by Christians. Yet the effort to deliver labor and man from the domination of money is an outgrowth of the currents released in the world by the preaching of the Gospel, such as the effort to abolish servitude and the effort to bring about the recognition of the rights of the human person.

Christ sent the sword to the heart of human history. The human race will emerge from the era of great sufferings only when the activity of hidden stimulation, by means of which the Christian spirit moves along and toils at bloody cost in the night of earthly history, will have joined with the activity of illumination, by means of which the Christian spirit sets souls up in the truth and life of the kingdom of God. It is not at the end of the present war that this goal will be reached. But the present war reveals to us, as by an apocalyptic sign, the direction in which we must move; and peace, if peace is won, will denote that the creative forces in motion within human history are decidedly set in this direction.

The Christian spirit is threatened today in its very existence by implacable enemies, fanatics of race and blood, of pride, domination and hate. At the core of the horrible ordeal, everything indicates that in the depths of human conscience a powerful religious renewal is in preparation, which concerns and which will restore to their vital sources all the persecuted, all the believers of the great Judeo-Christian family, not only the faithful of the Catholic Church and those of the Protestant Churches, but also those of Judaism, whose abandonment to nameless suffering and iniquity, and to

the sword of vile exterminators would be an un-
bearable scandal for the soul if we did not see in
it a terrible reminder of the promises of their God.
And it is by working in the density of the life of
the world, in an attempt to transform temporal existence, that this spiritual renewal, whatever be
the irreducible division that it involves on the dog-
matic and religious plane, will exercise a common
action and will bring forth common fruits.

Democracy, too, is threatened in its very existence, and by the same enemies. Although its roots
are evangelical, although it springs from that process of hidden stimulation mentioned above, and by
means of which Christianity dimly activates earthly
history, it is nonetheless by aligning itself with
erroneous ideologies and with aberrant tendencies
that it manifested itself in the world. Neither Locke
nor Jean-Jacques Rousseau nor the Encyclopedists
can pass as thinkers faithful to the integrity of the
Christian trust. Here too everything indicates that
a great renewal of the spirit is taking place which
tends to restore democracy to its true essence and
purify its principles. The re-examination of values
and the heroic effort which might have saved the
democracies from war, if they had been attempted

in time, are taking place and will take place in the midst of the ruins.

Thus in the fearful historical upheaval, on which the Pagan Empire is staking its all to liquidate at the same stroke Christianity and democracy, the chances of religion, conscience and civilization coincide with those of freedom; freedom's chances coincide with those of the evangelical message.

EVANGELICAL INSPIRATION AND THE SECULAR CONSCIENCE

I COMPARED above the spiritual essence and the genuine principle of democracy to a tree whose sap is healthy and which has been overgrown by parasites. When at the end of the eighteenth century the Rights of Man were proclaimed in America and in France, and the peoples bidden to partake of the ideal of Liberty, Equality and Fraternity, a great challenge of the people, of the plain man, of the spirit of childhood and faith, and at the same time of an ideal of universal generosity, was hurled in the political domain itself at the mighty of this world and their experienced skepticism. The evangelical impulse which thus erupted bore the imprint of a secularized Christianity; rationalist philosophy added to it illusions—which quickly became bloody—and assured mankind that the goodness of nature and reason alone would suffice for the coming of the great promise of justice and peace. But through these illusions the heart of man sensed a sacred truth: that the energies of the Gospel must pass into temporal life; that the good tidings heralded as throwing open heaven and eternal life ask also to transform the life of earthly societies in the very midst of its woes and its contradictions, that there are in the message of the Gospel political and social implications which must at all cost be unfurled in history.

And do you think that old Christian peoples would have gone to the trouble of starting revolutions and massacres, would have set out with all their household and the heritage of their labor, if it had not been for the promised and so long awaited beatitudes? If it is a mirage to believe them within reach of the hand, it is not a mirage to set out after them. The Middle Ages sought with the Holy Empire to erect a fortress for God on earth. Today the poor and the oppressed are setting out for the land of justice and fraternity. To have awakened and then betrayed such a hope is a measure of the failure of the modern world. It would be a worse failure to renounce this hope, and to seek to uproot it from men's hearts. Hard experience has taught us that the kingdom of God is not meant for earthly history, but at the same time we have become aware of this crucial truth that it must be enigmatically prepared in the midst of the pains of earthly history.

Christianity announced to the peoples the kingdom of God and the life to come; it has taught them the unity of the human race, the natural equality of all men, children of the same God and redeemed by the same Christ, the inalienable dignity of every soul fashioned in the image of God, the dignity of labor and the dignity of the poor, the primacy of inner values and of good will over external values, the inviolability of consciences, the exact vigilance of God's justice and providence over the great and the small. It has taught them the obligation imposed on those who govern and on those who have possessions to govern in justice, as ministers of God, and to manage the goods entrusted to them to the common advantage, as God's stewards, the submission of all to the law of work and the call to all to share in the freedom of the sons of God. It has taught them the sanctity of truth and the power of the Spirit, the communion of the saints, the divine supremacy of redeeming love and mercy, and the law of brotherly love which reaches out to all, even to those who are our enemies, because all men, to whatever social group, race, nation or class they may belong, are members of God's family and adopted brothers of the Son of God. Christianity proclaimed that where love and charity are, there God is; and that it is up to us to make every man our neighbor, by loving him as ourselves and by having compassion for him, that is, in a sense, by dying unto ourselves for his sake. Christ cursed the rich and the Pharisees. He promised the poor, and those who suffer persecution for the sake of justice, that they shall inherit the kingdom of heaven, the meek that they shall inherit the earth, those who mourn that they shall be comforted, those that hunger and thirst after justice that they shall be satisfied, the merciful that they shall obtain mercy, the pure in heart that they shall see God, the peace-makers that they shall be called sons of God. He declared that everything that is done to the meanest of His brothers is done to Him, He gave to His disciples the new commandment: to love one another as He Himself has loved them.

What then are the thoughts and aspirations which the Christian message has by degrees awakened in the depths of the conscience of peoples, and which moved along underground for centuries before becoming manifest? However misunderstood and distorted they may have become in the course of this hidden journey in the secular conscience, what are those truths of evangelical origin which this conscience henceforth linked and identified with the very idea of civilization?

If we seek to consider them in themselves, separating them from any erroneous contexts, we would say that by virtue of the hidden work of evangelical inspiration, the secular conscience has understood that human history does not go around in circles, but is set toward a goal and moves in a certain direction. Progress is not automatic and necessary, but threatened and thwarted; progress is not due to an advent of pure reason which would invalidate the entire heritage of the past, it is rather this very heritage which increases while it groans under the labor of all the human and divine energies in man. Progress does not lead to the recovery of Paradise by Revolution tomorrow, it tends to the carrying over of the structures of conscience and the structures of human life to better states, and this all through history up to the advent of the kingdom of God and the land of the resurrected, which is beyond history. Whether or not you believe in this advent, it is toward it that you are moving, if you believe in the forward march of humanity. And what at any rate has been gained for the secular conscience, if it does not veer to barbarism, is faith in the forward march of humanity.

Under the often misunderstood but active inspiration of the Gospel, the secular conscience has understood the dignity of the human person and has understood that the person, while being a part of the State, yet transcends the State, because of the inviolable mystery of his spiritual freedom and because of his call to the attainment of supraworldly possessions. The State's reason for existing is to help him in the acquisition of these possessions and of a truly human life. What has been gained for the secular conscience, if it does not veer to barbarism, is faith in the rights of the human person, as a human person, as a civic person, as a person engaged in social and economic life and as a working person; and it is faith in justice as a necessary foundation for common life, and as an essential property of the law, which is not a law if it is unjust. Proudhon believed that thirst for justice is the privilege of Revolution, and the object of attentive dread for the Church. The thirst for justice was imprinted in the soul of the Christian ages by the Gospel and the Church; it is from the Gospel and the Church that we learned to obey only if it is just to do so.

Under the inspiration of the Gospel at work in history, the secular conscience has understood the dignity of the people and of the common man. Faithful people, God's little people, kingly people, called to share in the work of Christ; people in the sense of the community of the citizens of a country, united under just laws; people in the sense of the community of manual labor and of the stock and resource of humanity in those who toil close to nature—the notion of the people which the secular conscience has gradually formed, stems from the meeting and mingling of all these elements, and it is from the heritage of Christendom that this notion proceeds. The people are not God, the people do not have infallible reason and virtues without flaw, the will of the people or the spirit of the people is not the rule which decides what is just or unjust.

But the people make up the slowly prepared and fashioned body of common humanity, the living patrimony of the common gifts and the common promises made to God's creature—which are more profound and more essential than all the additional privileges and the social distinctions—and of the equal dignity and equal weakness of all as members of the human race. It is on the condition of existing in communion with the people that all efforts bear fruit in temporal history, and that the inspirational leadership which the people need keeps both its strength and its legitimacy. Awakened to a consciousness of himself by the movement of civilization, the man of common humanity knows today that his day has dawned, if only he triumphs over totalitarian corruption and is not devoured by it; and he knows that the idea of a caste, of a class or a race hereditarily constituted as ruling and dominant must give way to the notion of a community of free men, equal in rights and in labor, and to the notion of an élite of the mind and of labor which stems from the people without cutting itself off from them, and which would truly be the flower and luxury of their vital energies. What has been gained for the secular conscience, if it does not veer to barbarism, is the sense of men's equality in nature and the relative equality which justice must establish among them, and the conviction that by means of the functional inequalities demanded by social life, equality must be re-established on a higher level, and must fructify in everyone's possibility of acceding to a life worthy of man, in everyone's assured enjoyment of the elementary possessions, both material and spiritual, of such a life, and in the true participation of each one, according to his capabilities and his worth, in the common task and the common heritage of civilization.

By virtue of the hidden work of evangelical inspiration, the secular conscience has understood that the authority of the rulers, by the very fact that it emanates from the author of human nature, is addressed to free men who do not belong to a master, and is exercised by virtue of the consent of the governed. The dictates of authority are binding in conscience because authority has its source in God; but from the very fact that authority has its source in God and not in man, no man and no particular group of men has in itself the right to rule others. The leaders of the people receive this right from the creative and conservative principle

of nature through the channels of nature itself, that
is, through the consent or will of the people or of
the body of the community, through which authority always passes before being invested in the
leaders. And it is as vicars or representatives of the
multitude that the holders of authority lead the
multitude, and it is toward the common good of the
multitude that they must lead it. It is contrary to
nature for men, members of the same species, all
equal before God and death, to be simple tools of
political power—tools of a dictator, the only human person among a flock of organized slaves, or
tools of a paternalist power, the only adult among
a regiment of children. Once the man of common
humanity has understood that he is born with the
right to conduct his own life by himself, as a being
responsible for his acts before God and the law of
the community, how can the people be expected to
obey those who govern unless it is because the latter
have received from the people themselves the cus-
tody of the people's common good? What has been
gained for the secular conscience, if it does not veer
to barbarism, is the conviction that authority,
or the right to exercise power, is held by the rulers
of the earthly community only because the com-

mon consent has been manifested in them, and because they have received their trust from the people; and it is the conviction that the normal state to which human societies ought to aspire is a state in which the people will act as grown-ups or those come of age in political life.

By virtue of the hidden work of evangelical inspiration the secular conscience has understood that the political realm and the flesh and blood paraphernalia of the things that are Caesar's must nevertheless be subject to God and to justice, it has understood that the entire art of domination and all the crimes which the princes and the heads of nations carry out to conquer and consolidate their power can certainly give them power but inevitably turn out for the misfortune of the peoples. Christianity cast the net of the Gospel upon the Pagan Empire and the Pagan Empire died of it, for there is no quarter given between the evangelical law of the Son of God and the law of the Empire which sets itself up as God. Once man has understood that in the truth of things politics depends upon morality because its aim is the human good of the community, once he has understood that political life must conform to natural law and, according to the special conditions of its temporal object, even to the law of the Gospel, he sees at the same moment that to call for justice and law in politics is to call for a great revolution which will substitute for the power politics of the masters, men, States or nations, the politics of the common good over which the people themselves must watch as the chief interested parties. A community of free men cannot live if its spiritual base is not solely law. Machiavellianism and the politics of domination, in the sight of which justice and law are a sure means of ruining everything, are the born enemies of a community of free men. What has been gained for the secular conscience, if it does not veer to barbarism, is the condemnation of the politics of domination and of iniquitous and perverse means in the guidance of nations, the profound feeling that justice fosters order and injustice the worst disorder, and the conviction that the cause of the welfare and freedom of the people and the cause of political justice are substantially linked.

Under the often misunderstood or disfigured but active inspiration of the Gospel, the secular conscience has awakened not only to the dignity of the human person, but also to the aspirations and the élan which are at work in his depths. The person, in itself a root of independence, but immersed in the constraints emanating from material nature within and outside man, tends to transcend these constraints and gain freedom of autonomy and expansion. In the very realm of spiritual life the message of the Gospel has revealed to the human person that he is called to the perfect freedom of those who have become a single spirit and love with God, but in the realm of temporal life it is the natural aspiration of the person to liberation from misery, servitude, and the exploitation of man by man, that the repercussions of the Gospel's message were to stimulate. When you know that we are all made for blessedness, death no longer holds any terror; but you cannot become resigned to the oppression and enslavement of your brothers, and you aspire, for the earthly life of humanity, to a state of emancipation consonant with the dignity of this life. What has been gained for the secular conscience, if it does not veer to barbarism, is the sense of freedom, and the conviction that the forward march of human societies is a march toward the conquest of a freedom consonant with the vocation of our nature.

Finally under the inspiration of the Gospel at

work in history, the secular conscience has understood that in the misfortunes and suffering of our existence, crushed by the iron laws of biological necessity and by the weight of the pride, injustice and wickedness of men, a single principle of liberation, a single principle of hope, a single principle of peace can stir up the mass of servitude and iniquity and triumph over it, because this principle comes down to us from the creative source of the world, stronger than the world: that brotherly love whose law was promulgated by the Gospel to the scandal of the mighty, and which is, as the Christian well knows, God's own charity diffused into the hearts of men. And the secular conscience has understood that in the temporal social and political order itself, not only is civic friendship, as the ancient philosophers knew it, the soul and the constitutive link of the social community (if justice is first of all an essential requirement, it is as a necessary condition which makes friendship possible), but this very friendship between citizens cannot prevail in actual fact within the social group if a stronger and more universal love, brotherly love, is not instilled in it, and if civic friendship, itself becoming brotherhood, does not overflow the bounds of the social group to extend to the entire human race. Once the heart of man has felt the freshness of that terrible hope, it is troubled for all time. If it fails to recognize its supra-human origins and exigencies, this hope runs the risk of becoming perverted and of changing into violence to impose upon all "brotherhood or death." But woe to us if we scorn this hope itself, and succeed in delivering the human race from the promise of brotherhood. The human race has been exalted by it, it will give it up only at the cost of becoming more fierce than before. This hope is holy in itself, it corresponds to the deepest and most ineradicable desires of human nature; it places souls in a communion of pain and longing with all the oppressed and the persecuted; it calls for heroism; it has a divine power for transforming human history. What has been gained for the secular conscience, if it does not veer to barbarism, is faith in the brotherhood of man, a sense of the social duty of compassion for mankind in the person of the weak and the suffering, the conviction that the political work par excellence is that of rendering common life better and more brotherly, and of working so as to make of the structure of laws, institutions and customs of this common life a house for brothers to live in.

THE TRUE ESSENCE OF DEMOCRACY

THE IDEAS and the aspirations of which I have just spoken characterize the democratic state of mind and the democratic philosophy of man and society. And it is under the influence of the evangelical ferment at work in the world that they took shape in the secular conscience. During the nineteenth century and particularly in Europe, as a consequence of the most absurd of historical contradictions, these ideas and aspirations were involved in a so-called philosophy of the emancipation of thought which drained them of all substance, disavowed and disintegrated them, all the while pretending to "put out the stars" in the name of science,[1] and to make of man a soulless ape for whom the accidents of zoölogical mutations turned out favorably. In themselves, however, these ideas and these aspirations remained and will always remain essentially linked

---

[1] Words used by a French Prime Minister, René Viviani, in a famous speech to Parliament.

to the Christian message and to the action of hidden stimulation which this message exercises in the depths of the secular conscience of the world.

That is why I said above that the democratic impulse burst forth in history as a temporal manifestation of the inspiration of the Gospel. Statesmen know this well, and it is not without reason that in their defense of democracy they are today invoking the Sermon on the Mount. In his message of January 4, 1939, which has been said to contain "the outline of that reconstruction in their moral philosophy which the democracies must undertake if they are to survive," [2] President Roosevelt stressed the fact that democracy, respect for the human person, for liberty, and for international good faith find their soundest foundation in religion and furnish religion with its best guarantees. He recently affirmed that "we [the United Nations] shall seek . . . the establishment of an international order in which the spirit of Christ shall rule the hearts of men and of nations." [3]

In an important speech delivered on May 8,

[2] Walter Lippmann, *New York Herald Tribune*, January 7, 1939.

[3] Letter to the American Bishops, *Catholic News*, January 17, 1942.

1942, Henry A. Wallace, the Vice-President of the United States, declared in turn: "The Idea of freedom . . . is derived from the Bible with its extraordinary emphasis on the dignity of the individual. Democracy is the only true political expression of Christianity." [4] Toward the close of his life, Chateaubriand had expressed the same thought. And in his book, *The Two Sources of Morality and Religion*, Henri Bergson also stated that because in the republican slogan "the essential thing is fraternity," we must state that "democracy is evangelical in essence." To the misfortune and the confusion of ideas of the modern world, Rousseau and Kant dressed democratic thought up in their sentimental and philosophical formulas. We know, however, "how much Kant owed to his pietism, and Rousseau to an interplay of Protestantism and Catholicism." [5] The sources of the democratic ideal must be sought many centuries before Kant and Rousseau.

Not only does the democratic state of mind stem from the inspiration of the Gospel, but it cannot

[4] *The Price of Free World Victory,* speech delivered on May 8, 1942 before the Free World Association.

[5] Henri Bergson, *The Two Sources of Morality and Religion,* p. 243, English edition.

exist without it. To keep faith in the forward march of humanity despite all the temptations to despair of man that are furnished by history, and particularly contemporary history; to have faith in the dignity of the person and of common humanity, in human rights and in justice—that is, in essentially spiritual values; to have, not in formulas but in reality, the sense of and respect for the dignity of the people, which is a spiritual dignity and is revealed to whoever knows how to love it; to sustain and revive the sense of equality without sinking into a leveling equalitarianism; to respect authority, knowing that its wielders are only men, like those they rule, and derive their trust from the consent or the will of the people whose vicars or representatives they are; to believe in the sanctity of law and in the efficacious virtue—efficacious at long range —of political justice in face of the scandalous triumphs of falsehood and violence; to have faith in liberty and in fraternity, an heroical inspiration and an heroical belief are needed which fortify and vivify reason, and which none other than Jesus of Nazareth brought forth in the world.

Let us also consider the immense burden of animality, of egoism, and of latent barbarism that men bear within themselves and which keeps social life still terribly far from achieving its truest and most elevated aims. Let us realize this fact that the part of instinct and irrational forces is even greater in communal existence than in individual existence, and that at the moment when the people enter into history by claiming their political and social majority, large portions of humanity remain in a state of immaturity or suffer from morbid complexes accumulated in the course of time, and are still no more than the rough draft or the preparation of that fruit of civilization which we call a people. Let us understand that in order to enjoy its privileges as an adult in political life without running the risk of failure a people must be able to act grown-up: then we will understand that the era has still not passed when for democracy itself force—righteous force—aside from its normal rôle in the policing of societies, must also play a subsidiary rôle of protecting against the return of the instinct of domination, exploitation or anarchic egoism. And above all we will understand that, with a view to curtailing as much as possible and eliminating by degrees these subsidiary functions of force, more than ever democracy needs the evangelical ferment in order to be realized and in order to endure. The lasting advent of the democratic state of mind and of the democratic philosophy of life requires the energies of the Gospel to penetrate secular existence, taming the irrational to reason and becoming embodied in the vital dynamism of the tendencies and instincts of nature, in order to fashion and stabilize in the depths of the subconscious those reflexes, habits and virtues without which the intellect which leads action fluctuates with the wind and wasting egoism prevails in man. It was Joseph de Maistre who said: "Wherever a religion other than the Christian religion holds sway, there slavery is sanctioned, and wherever the Christian religion weakens, the nation becomes, in exact proportion, less capable of general liberty. . . . Government alone cannot govern, it needs either slavery which reduces the number of active wills in the State, or divine force, which by a kind of spiritual grafting, destroys the natural harshness of these wills, and enables them to work together without harm to one another." [6]

It is not enough for a population or a section of the population to have Christian faith and be docile

[6] *Le Pape,* Book III, Chapter 2.

to the ministers of religion in order to be in a position properly to judge political matters. If this population has no political experience, no taste for seeing clearly for itself nor a tradition of initiative and critical judgment, its position with respect to politics grows more complicated, for nothing is easier for political counterfeiters than to exploit good principles for purposes of deception, and nothing is more disastrous than good principles badly applied. And moreover nothing is easier for human weakness than to merge religion with prejudices of race, family or class, collective hatreds, passions of a clan and political phantoms which compensate for the rigors of individual discipline in a pious but insufficiently purified soul. Politics deal with matters and interests of the world and they depend upon passions natural to man and upon reason. But the point I wish to make here is that without goodness, love and charity, all that is best in us—even divine faith, but passions and reason much more so —turns in our hands to an unhappy use. The point is that right political experience cannot develop in people unless passions and reason are oriented by a solid basis of collective virtues, by faith and honor and thirst for justice. The point is that without the

evangelical instinct and the spiritual potential of a
living Christianity, political judgment and political
experience are ill protected against the illusions of
selfishness and fear; without courage, compassion
for mankind, and the spirit of sacrifice the ever-
thwarted advance toward an historical ideal of generosity and fraternity is not conceivable.

As Bergson has shown in his profound analyses,
it is the urge of a love infinitely stronger than the
philanthropy commended by philosophers which
caused human devotion to surmount the closed
borders of the natural social groups—family group
and national group—and extended it to the entire
human race, because this love is the life in us of the
very love which has created being and because it
truly makes of each human being our neighbor.
Without breaking the links of flesh and blood, of
self-interest, tradition and pride which are needed
by the body politic, and without destroying the
rigorous laws of existence and conservation of this
body politic, such a love extended to all men transcends and at the same time transforms from within
the very life of the group, and tends to integrate all
of humanity into a community of nations and
peoples in which men will be reconciled. For the
kingdom of God is not miserly, the communion

which is its supernatural privilege is not jealously guarded; it wants to spread and refract this communion outside its own limits, in the imperfect shapes and in the universe of conflicts, malice and bitter toil which make up the temporal realm. That is the deepest principle of the democratic ideal, which is the secular name for the ideal of Christendom. That is why, Bergson writes, "democracy is evangelical in essence and . . . its motive power is love." [7]

Yet in the same way it also appears that the democratic ideal runs against the grain of nature, whose law is not evangelical love. ". . . They were false democracies, those cities of antiquity, based on slavery, relieved by this fundamental iniquity of the biggest and most excruciating problems." [8] Democracy is a paradox and a challenge hurled at nature, at that thankless and wounded human nature whose original aspirations and reserves of grandeur it evokes. In the democratic ideal, and "in the democratic frame of mind" we must see, Bergson writes, "a great effort running against the grain of nature": [9] which does not mean an effort contrary to nature, but an effort to straighten na-

[7] Henri Bergson, *op. cit.*, p. 243.
[8] *Ibid.*
[9] *Ibid.*

ture, an effort linked to the developments of reason and justice and which must take place in history under the influence of the Christian leaven; an effort which requires that nature and the temporal order be elevated by the action of this leaven within their own realm, in the realm of civilization's movement. If the development of machinery and the great conquests which we have seen in the realm of matter and technique demand "an increment of soul" in order to become true instruments of liberation, it is also by means of this increment of soul that democracy will be realized. Its progress is bound up with the spiritualization of secular existence.

The democratic philosophy of man and society has faith in the resources and the vocation of human nature. In the great adventure of our life and our history it is placing its stakes on justice and generosity. It is therefore betting on heroism and the spiritual energies. This idealism runs all the risks if it does not take its source sufficiently high and if at the same stroke it misjudges the harsh natural realities at the heart of which it must work, for then it dares not face the existence and power of evil because it does not feel within itself the strength to overcome them. But if it truly understands the dignity of man and his vocation; if it is cognizant of the power of truth and the power of love; if it has respect for the soul and an awareness of the soul's grandeur; if at the top of the scale of values it places the workings of the spirit and of freedom; and if it knows that the pursuit of happiness is mysteriously linked to self-sacrifice, because it is above all the pursuit of the fulfillment of the human being in love, and because material goods and abundance in communal life are to be sought first of all as the conditions and means of such a goal; if it knows that the work of temporal salvation and earthly emancipation of humanity is at one and the same time the work of a humanity ransomed for eternal life and of a Redeeming God whose blood passes into its veins, then the idealism inherent in democratic philosophy can face the fierceness of the laws of material nature, the weakness and the perversity of men and the reality of evil in the world, because it knows that there is in man and above man the wherewithal to overcome all that. Indeed, all that will be overcome only amidst many impurities and imperfections. That is precisely why we must want all the more strongly to overcome it.

The essential characteristics of the democratic philosophy of man and society, or of the humanist political philosophy, stand forth with the greatest clarity in their opposition to the slave philosophy. This humanist political philosophy may be identified by the features which I stressed above: inalienable rights of the person, equality, political rights of the people whose consent is implied by any political régime and whose rulers rule as vicars of the people, absolute primacy of the relations of justice and law at the base of society, and an ideal not of war, prestige or power, but of the amelioration and emancipation of human life—the ideal of fraternity. For this philosophy the political task is *par excellence* a task of civilization and culture; it tends above all to provide the common good of the multitude in such a way that the concrete person, not only within the category of the privileged, but in the whole mass, truly accedes to the measure of independence which is compatible with civilized life and which is assured alike by the economic guarantees of labor and property, political rights, civic virtues and the cultivation of the mind. The democratic philosophy thrives on the unceasing work of invention, criticism and demands of individual conscience—it thrives on it and it would die of it if it were not also living on the unceasing gift of self which must correspond to this unceasing work of criticism and demand; running counter to the natural bent of man's imagination, it denies to the rulers the right to consider themselves and be considered a superior race, and wills nevertheless that their authority be respected on a juridical basis. It does not admit that the State is a transcendent power incorporating within itself all authority and imposed from above upon human life; it demands that autonomous organs, in possession of authority commensurate with their function, emanate spontaneously from the civil community and from the tension existing between its diverse activities, and that the State—controlled by the nation—be nothing more than the highest organ of regulation, whose object is the common good as it concerns the totality as such.

Are we called upon now to define that form of government to which the principles of the humanist political philosophy naturally tend? This philosophy maintains that the human person as such is called upon to participate in political life and that the political rights of a community of free men must be firmly secured. That is why it claims the right of suffrage for all adult citizens, of whatever race and social condition, and demands also that a juridically formulated constitution determine the basic laws of the régime under which the people deliberately resolve to place their political life. The principles of the democratic philosophy of man and society can adjust themselves to a (constitutional) system of monarchic or oligarchic government. But by right, as in fact, it is to the republican system that these principles tend as their most normal expression—to a system of government which must link and attune to the democratic dominant of freedom and the progressive enfranchisement of the human being, the qualities of oneness and of the differentiation of values, which were the prevailing features of the monarchic régime and the aristocratic régime since transcended, and in which the legislative power must be exercised by the representatives of the people, and the executive power by delegates who are directly or indirectly appointed by the people and whose conduct of affairs is controlled by them.

According to the popular saying, the democratic régime is described as the régime of the sovereignty of the people. This expression is ambiguous, for in truth there is no sovereign nor absolute master in a democracy. It would be better to say that democracy is the régime wherein the people enjoy their social and political majority and exercise it to conduct their own affairs; or better still to say that democracy is "the government of the people, by the people, for the people." Which means that the people are then governed by men whom they themselves have chosen for functions of a determined nature and duration, and over whose management they maintain a regular control, first of all by means of their representatives and the assemblies thus constituted.

The error of individualistic liberalism lay in denying in principle to those elected by the people every real right of command, on the pretext that everyone must "obey himself alone": these elected officers then became holders of a power without authority, and at the very moment that they were governing the people, they were obliged to make the people believe them mere passive tools of the people. In reality they receive their charge from the people and must govern in communion with them, but they hold real authority within the limits of their functions. Another error lay in reducing the community to an atomized mass of individuals confronted with an all-powerful State in which the will of each one was supposed to engulf and annihilate itself and mystically come to life again in the form of the general will; the error lay furthermore in excluding the existence and the autonomy, the initiative and the rights proper to each group or community of a rank inferior to the State, and finally, in causing the very concept of common good and common task to vanish. These errors which correspond to the advent of the bourgeois class and ideology, far from becoming an integral part of democracy, are deadly to democracy. These errors paved the way to totalitarianism, as did complacency to mediocrity and the hegemony of political parties, which are not essential to democracy either, but which are the constant temptation of all democracies lacking spiritual vigor. By freeing itself from such errors, a new democracy will be restored to the genuine principles of democratic philosophy.

This new democracy will not come into being easily. Even the most just of wars is a crisis brought on by the process of *disintoxication,* and which may turn out badly. It breaks open all abscesses. We must burn out all the pre-war poisons and do away with those which the war itself will have produced. In depth this operation affects all the structures of civilization, in scope the entire world. Once the Pagan Empire has been laid waste, its putrefaction of moral nihilism, of sadistic brutality, and of frenzied ideas will not be swept away at one blow, nor yet the inexpiable hatreds that it will have awakened, nor the vast amount of cast-off and shameful illusions which its lackeys, put to flight, will have dropped along the road. We will also have to face ancient interests and ancient economic privileges everywhere defending themselves tenaciously; ancient ambitions and ancient errors still eager to prey on the democracies; and new risks emanating from hardened national instincts and blind claims of prestige, or from the desire to turn the misfortune of men to account for a gold mine of profits and for the hegemony of big business, or from the fancies of the ignorant who seek to refashion the map of the world according to the principles of geopolitics and organize the universe "rationally" without knowing that man has a soul. The intelligence of the best architects is baffled

when confronted with a civilization to be rebuilt;
a new international order to be established, restor-
ing their destinies not only to liberated Europe, but
to liberated China and emancipated India; a new
disposition, equitable for all men, to be found for
what we still call the Colonial Empires—and which
will not be found unless there truly prevail the
sense of moral responsibility toward the popula-
tions, of respect for their soul and their wishes, and
of true human fellowship with them. It is to be
hoped that a sufficiently extended period of trial
and adjustment, controlled by international agen-
cies, will give experience the time to enlighten
reason. In truth the democracies have to contend
at one and the same time with the Pagan Empire
and with themselves. They must triumph over
Hitler and over their own self-contradictions in the
social and spiritual realms. And not only must they
recover on the one hand their genuine social and
political impulse, and on the other hand their
genuine spiritual impulse, but they must reconcile
the two—and to that end get rid of bitter prejudices and ill-will.

THE NEW LEADERSHIP

THE MORE DIFFICULT this immense task appears, the more it should tempt men. Peoples are set in motion only for difficult things.

In all the nations today prostrate, especially in France, the leading classes have gone morally bankrupt. The failure of our world is *their* failure. The time has come to call upon the moral and spiritual reserves of the people, of common humanity—the last reserves of civilization—indissolubly in support of victory and reconstruction. And these moral and spiritual reserves are not a tool in the hands of those with authority; they are the very power, and the source of initiative, of men cognizant of their personal dignity and their responsibility.

The totalitarians have perverted the word people as they have perverted all the words of the language. The people is not that mass of human matter, de-personalized and blended into a single physical entity, a single energy and a single "spirit" of the powers of the earth, which the abominable racist mythology has invented and which they attempt to realize by dint of enslavement, and in whose name they perpetrate all their crimes. The people? They hate, scorn and fear the people; they seek not only to oppress them—it is the very reality of the people that they seek to obliterate from existence. The people are souls, human persons gathered together by common human tasks and by the common consciousness of the work that each one must do to have his place in the sun with his family and his friends, by a long experience of the trials and joys of a life devoid of glory, by a common fund of hereditary wisdom amassed in the minds of the hard-working, by human sentiments, human traditions and human instincts which foster in each one, close to nature, a personal effort, however restricted it may be, of reason and freedom. The people comprise the patient thrust of the activities of the human intellect and human labor multiplying in individual lives at the ground level of civilized existence.

In the same way, what I refer to as the man of common humanity is not the good savage nor the abstract man, the solitary individual divested of all social patrimony. If there is anything that corresponds to this idea in actual existence, it is the social wastes which form the most errant and most miserable strata of the proletariat or of those classes in the process of being proletarianized. That man does not inspire me with confidence. He is the one who furnishes the dictators with their mobs and their executioners. What I call the man of common humanity, he in whom I have confidence, is the great multitude of men who, engaged in the moral and social structures of civilized existence, however humble these may be, and of those groups where the collective conscience awakens, perform the common tasks, the great elementary and anonymous work of human life, and are not tempted to think themselves a superior race—because their work is not signed and because they are the men of this people of which I have spoken, the plain people.

I do not share the romantic optimism which ascribes to the people a judgment which is always just and instincts which are always upright. I know too that they must be organized in order to express themselves and to act. But I maintain that the

tragic sophism of the reactionaries consists in con-
founding the behavior of a free people, acting
within the framework of its legitimate institutions,
with the bloody violence of crowds crazed by collective passions, by those collective passions which
totalitarian propaganda diabolically kindles. I say
that the man of common humanity is not possessed
of a less sound judgment and less equitable instincts
than those social categories which believe themselves superior, and that, taken all in all—not because he is more intelligent but because he is less
tempted—he has less chance of going astray in the
major issues which concern him, the common man,
than the so-called élite of informed and competent
and rich and high-born and highly cultivated or
highly cunning persons who have cut themselves
off from the people, and whose political imbecility,
baseness of soul, and corruption are today astound-
ing the universe. I say that today in all of Europe
and especially in France the people are letting
themselves be less fooled by the trickery of the
German new order, and have better preserved
honor, and are struggling against the oppressor
more courageously than many politicians, indus-
trialists and high civil and military functionaries.

I say that the inspirational leadership which the people need must always live in communion with this people which is giving indefatigably of its labor and its blood. Now, whether we will or no, and in accordance with an essential postulate of democratic thought, the new leadership must come forth from the depths of the nations. It will be composed of the working and peasant élite, together with the elements of the former leading classes which have decided to work with the people. The essential problem of reconstruction is not a problem of plans, it is a problem of men, the problem of the new leadership to come. It is not by self-appointment that these leaders will become qualified. May they be appointed by heroism and devotion! In so far as the French nation is concerned, its new guides and its new institutions, the institutions of the Fourth Republic, will arise from the common experience and the common faith of those who have not despaired of the people and the nation, and will stem from the work of selection and human preparation that these mournful years of hidden and fearful struggle will have effected in the French youth.

The task to be accomplished in the midst of the

ruins, the repairs in the elementary structures of human life, and even the great enterprises of world-wide reconstruction, require first of all a return to simplicity of vision. Once true perspective has been exposed to a simple movement of the heart, to a simple intuition of the intellect, the rest is the work of common sense and courage, experience and generosity. Truly it is not the principles and the ideas which are lacking. In the best sections of the youth, the work of intellectual and moral reform had been under way for several years. But the new democratic philosophy will be fully elaborated in performance alone. Everything depends on the new leaders. The world has desperate need of them.

THE COMMUNIST PROBLEM

IF I AM ASKED what the attitude of these new leaders will be toward Communists and toward the new situation created on the one hand by the heroism of the Russian people and by their unheard-of sacrifices, on the other hand by the action which the Communists, side by side with the other groups of resistance, are leading against the oppressor in the occupied countries, and by the frenzy of persecution of the pro-Nazi rulers who are turning Communists into martyrs for their country and who term as Communists all those who are fighting for freedom, I would say that if I see in Nazism the final stage of an implacable reaction against the democratic principle and against the Christian principle all in one, I see in Communism the final stage in the inner destruction of the democratic principle due to the rejection of the Christian principle. Communism is

situated along the line of march of man's emancipation—at the historic convergence of the principles of error which are mingled with this march.
As a doctrine it is unchangeable and logically
bound up with atheism. If it were nothing more
than an economic system, it would be possible to
conceive, whatever be the intrinsic value of such
a system, of a Christian Communism—something
of the sort was seen in the early Christian com-
munities, as today in the religious orders. But Communism is not an economic system alone, it is a
philosophy of life based on a coherent and absolute rejection of divine transcendence, a discipline
of life and a mysticism of integral revolutionary
materialism. Still, because of the very existence
of the new situation just mentioned and the historical turnovers it involves, and because Communism is a totalitarian and atheistic catastrophe
of democracy itself and of the humanistic impulse
of democracy (whereas racism is an anti-democratic spurt based on the worship of violence and
the denial of the oneness of the human race), there
is yet a chance for a general righting of democratic thought and action to reinstate in democracy, in a respect for the things of the soul, in the

love of freedom and the sense of the dignity of the person—not indeed Marxist orthodoxy and the discipline of the Communist Party—but many Communists of sensibility and many persons who are favorably disposed to Communism by the revolt against social injustice. An indication of the possibility of such changes in men and in concrete existence may be found in the practical giving way already experienced in the Soviet Union by Marxist dogma, in the cessation at the present time of the anti-religious campaign and in the government-sponsored re-establishment of the Orthodox Church, in the prayers for victory of the faithful, in the admirable passion which today animates the Russian people in the defense of their wounded land and which is neither specifically communistic nor specifically atheistic, but which is merely a return to the source of human grandeur.

This chance is the only one open to us with respect to the Communist problem. It would be less uncertain if the generosity of the other peoples, and of the Christians in the world, were to make itself known in time to help the Russian people, not only to smash the effort of the German armies, but also to effect their re-entrance into the

Western community and into regenerated democracy.[1]

In principle there are three attitudes possible with regard to the Communists. We can seek to destroy them by force, machine-guns and concentration camps, and invoke the demons of triumphant German Racism, the Pagan Empire and Fascism against them. This attitude, dictated not by a solicitude for those human and divine values which are threatened by Communism, but by the blind fear of losing one's possessions or the prestige of one's class, is a betrayal of civilization.

We can give way to them and constitute together with them a single political "front" which they can control from without and from within, or crush one day to their own advantage. Which means, unless one is a victim of incurable illusions, accepting beforehand the risk of turning the peoples over to the hegemony of the Communists or to civil

[1] It should be pointed out, moreover, that the case of the Soviet Union and the case of the Communist Party in the other nations are quite different. Russia has experienced her Communist revolution and has more or less digested it; she seems now mainly concerned with preserving what she has, and with her national interests. The Communists in the other nations have not yet achieved their aims and are eager to experience success of their own; they don't want to preserve, but to conquer. The problems of internal policy with regard to them will thus, probably, arouse more difficulties than will the problems of external policy with regard to the Soviet Union.

strife. This attitude is another betrayal, for on the one hand it furnishes both pretext and stimulation to the former attitude, and on the other hand it sacrifices the future of civilization to the anxiety of obtaining more rapid success in the political struggle—success which is in reality ephemeral.

Finally, we can grasp the fact that Communists are not Communism, and that, at the cost of blood shed in the cause of common liberation, they have openly won the right to take part in the work of reconstruction as companions in arms, and at the same time we can refuse all offers of a single political front, all regimentation and all submission to party maneuvers. While demanding that the strength of the laws which protect freedom must be opposed •to schemes of violence, from whatever quarter they may come, this attitude requires that we frankly accept the cooperation of the Communists and their participation in the common task, but that we maintain complete autonomy with regard to them. Then we would have an opportunity of seeing the struggle between Communism and its opponents transformed into competition—doubtless bitter—in the constructive work to be done. In such a case the effort of the opponents of Communism would be based upon the conviction that success in the good and in justice and in every endeavor to alleviate human distress bears witness unto itself, and that a democracy fully resolved upon social justice and the changes which it demands, determined to put an end to the hegemony of money, animated and penetrated from all sides by an heroic spiritual flame, is not only in a position to rid Communism of its pretexts, but has also the power to draw in its wake and restore to its own ideal the greatest number of those who were attracted to Communism.

This attitude is the one which Pope Pius XI, perhaps with prophetic instinct, recommended to Christians toward the close of his life, weeping with pain and compassion. In December 1937 he said to the bishops of France: "French Catholics are often told of the 'proffered hand' . . . This hand which is held out to us, are we in a position to grasp it? I would it were so: a proffered hand is not to be refused, but it must not be accepted to the prejudice of truth. Truth is God, and God cannot be sacrificed. But those who speak of a proffered hand do not make themselves clear on this score. Their speech contains confusion and obscurity which must be dispelled. Let us therefore grasp their proffered hand, but in order that we may draw them to Christ's divine doctrine. And how are we to lead them to this doctrine? By expounding it to them? No. By living it, in all its goodness. . . .

"Christ did not make many conquests by preaching the truth: it led Him to the cross. It was through charity that He won souls and led them in His train. Nor is there any other way for us to win them. Look at the missionaries: by what means do they convert the unbelievers? By the good that they disseminate. You will convert those who are seduced by Communist doctrines in proportion as you show them that faith in Christ and love of Christ inspire devotion and goodness, in proportion as you show them that nowhere else can there be found a like source of charity.

"Stress this point. Oh, I well know that you are already doing a great deal in this respect, you and your faithful, but you must do more and better, and reach even to sacrifice. You have not forgotten St. Ambrose who asked that even the holy vases be sold so as to relieve human distress." [1]

What the Pope recommended on the religious

[1] *L'Aube,* December 15, 1937.

plane is also of value on the civic plane, but is possible here only if the charity of which he spoke really burns in our hearts. This is the attitude of evangelical love and generosity. History has launched us in an apocalypse where we are no longer permitted to shut our ears to the Gospel. A choice has to be made. Everything must be staked on hatred, or cowardice, or love.

Without seeking to prejudice unforeseen historical circumstances and accidents, there is reason to believe that this third attitude will be adopted by the new leadership in the liberated countries of the world.

AN HEROIC HUMANISM

IT HAS BEEN SAID and said again with reason that the present war is an international civil war, and that it is a revolution. It may be won from a military standpoint before it has been truly won. It is possible, and in truth this would be more normal, that it will be won from a military standpoint only when it has been truly won, won from a revolutionary standpoint. In any event it will not be truly won until the concrete outline for a new spiritual and social world will have made its appearance in history. In order to avoid a civil war which would follow upon this war, in order for the close of this war between nations to be at the same time the close of civil war within nations, this outline of a new world must be elaborated and must prevail in the very midst of the war.

The French people, defeated, betrayed, humiliated and oppressed, are placed by their very misfortune at the crucial point of the problem. With the Germans on their territory and with Hitler's collaborators in their government, they are suffering and living the tragedy in its most excruciating depths. If the force of their political instinct and the renewals of the spirit effected in the night of their suffering is equal to the violence of their disgust and their anger, they will be able to find in their terrible experience the wherewithal to help the world discover those new things which the world needs. And it is not alone by means of the retrieved national strength and integrity, it is also by means of a testimony of universal scope and a renewed spiritual and moral mission which would introduce everywhere the leaven which quickens the mass, that France will be restored to her historic vocation.

I am not naïve enough to believe that these things can be done easily, nor that they must inevitably be done, nor that the internal conflicts will be surmounted without trouble. Still the reasons for hoping are real. The old easy-going policy and many outmoded follies have been liquidated. The whole false order of slavery, which under other circumstances it might have taken a great deal of time to unmask, dishonored itself in a flash; the

Vichy régime will drag down with it the forces and ideas which threatened to prove an obstacle to, and a betrayal of, a true renewal, and which, in actual fact, have betrayed and sullied the most beautiful kingdom under the skies. The need for a fundamental transformation of the economic and social system is recognized everywhere, at the same time that there awakens a new republican enthusiasm, a desire for simplicity in a common life of work, and a well-considered will to the real liberation of the person and the groups in which it is enmeshed. Despite the serious dangers to which the myth of Marshal Pétain exposed the Church of France, the vital forces of the latter maintained the spirit of resistance in the depths of the country: in February 1942, anti-Semitism was denounced and condemned in the sermons preached by the clergy; the savage anti-Jewish persecution, since decreed by Laval, has stirred up in the Christian conscience a vast wave of indignation which has been translated into admirable acts and which has been sanctioned by the religious leaders, both Catholic and Protestant. The Catholic youth intrepidly militates for liberty; it wants a vitally and really—not decoratively—Christian community without a shadow of that "clericalism of which the Church disapproves and which we do not want at any price," as the Archbishop of Toulouse stated three years ago. Public opinion has understood that in order to escape from the base frivolity and the infamous weaknesses of politicians who were not all bad, but whose inner life was dust, we must exact from our leaders moral consistency, the strength of one who acts on principles, and not honesty alone, but virtue. Though it is probable that in the first days of reconstruction the State will have to control many things, Frenchmen have acquired a horror of statism, and everything leads us to believe that the spirit which will direct the work of restoration will tend toward forms of political and social life in which an organic pluralism will put an end in the nation to the omnipotence of the State, whereas those institutions which will cause cooperation to prevail in Europe and in the world, will put an end in the community of the peoples to the absolute sovereignty of national States.

There is one thing that Europe knows well, that she knows even too well; that is the tragic meaning of life. After a thousand years of suffering she has learned to know what man is and at what cost the slightest progress is accomplished. The experience thus acquired is a treasure of tears. It makes her run the risk of skepticism, but the experience of skepticism too which she had with her pre-war leaders and which she is having today with the leprosy of her collaborationists furnished her with proof that skepticism would dig her grave. If she knows the tragic meaning of life, she also knows the meaning of heroism, she knows that heroism alone surmounts tragedy.

There is one thing that America knows well, and that she teaches as a great and precious lesson to those who come into contact with her amazing adventure: that is the value and dignity of the man of common humanity, the value and dignity of the people. According to the popular phrase of the day, what we know as the *common man* is here neither servile nor arrogant. He has a feeling for the dignity of human existence and he exists in the collective consciousness of each one's worth. In forms so simply human that the pretentious and the pedantic are at pains to perceive it, we find there a spiritual conquest of immeasurable value. The mainspring of American civilization is this dignity of each one in daily existence, and it was in order to realize this more fully, not only on her own soil, but throughout the world, that America stepped out of her traditional isolation and faced war and that today she has set out for a new world. She knows that the man of common humanity has a right to the "pursuit of happiness"—a slogan which, if well-understood, denotes a series of implications: it denotes the pursuit of the primary conditions and primary possessions which are the prerequisites of a free life and whose denial, endured by so many multitudes, is a cruel wound in the flesh of humanity; it denotes the pursuit of the superior possessions of culture and the mind, the pursuit of liberation from want, from fear and from servitude; it denotes the pursuit of that freedom and that human plenitude bound up with the mastery of self which, in the imperfect order of temporal life, is the highest goal of civilization and which, in a superior order, asks to be perfectly realized by means of the spiritual transformation of the human being and which man can attain only by great love and the incessant gift of self. Here heroism is needed, not to overcome a tragedy, but to bring to a satisfactory close a wonderful adventure, begun for this country at the time of the Pilgrim Fathers and the pioneers and in the great days of the Declaration of Independence and the Revolutionary War.

Summoning all men to the pursuit of such happiness, if only we place it high enough and know the price it will cost, means undertaking the greatest of all temporal revolutions. And this has no meaning unless the call to the pursuit of happiness is indistinct from a call to heroism.

We have the right to call, not for a continual output of collective heroism, but for the common acceptance of an ideal of heroic life, upon the heroism of the plain man. The proof, sublime or monstrous, is before our eyes today. Millions of men are consenting to die for just or unjust causes, for a noble or abject ideal to which they have given their hearts and for which they are sacrificing everything they hold most dear. For iniquitous aggression or for just defense, victorious or vanquished, they are paying abundantly the price of blood. They are allowing their cities to be destroyed and burned, their women and children exposed to death, famine, torture. To all this they are constrained only in part by terror, or by the relentless laws of military discipline or civic discipline. To face all this it has been necessary for sources to rise from the very depths of their being, sources of misguided generosity or true generosity which give a more splendid lustre to the good, a human shade to evil.

Is it then impossible to turn these vast reserves of courage and endurance and the hidden instinct of sacrifice toward an austere and difficult work of human edification and brotherhood? Since in any case we have to give our lives, it is better to give them for our brothers than to reserve them for butchery. If the common life in which I am engaged is built upon injustice, one day I will have to look on with courage while the beasts skin me and my children alive. If common life tends toward justice, perhaps I ought to give up my skin and all the rest for justice: at least I shall have the expectation that my children will be happy, and courageous as well. It is far better to run oneself ragged for the good than to be run ragged for evil. These are simple facts; the time will come when the common conscience will understand them.

It is not a question of asking everyone to be ready for martyrdom his whole life through. The new leadership, yes, those men who will take up again for the modern peoples a task analogous to that of the old Christian orders which ransomed captives and defended the widow and the orphan, these men will be called upon in case of need to be martyrs to justice and brotherly friendship. But it is absurd to ask constant heroism of the great majority. The great majority knows hard work and daily courage; it has known them for centuries. What is asked is that in a civil community where social discipline will doubtless be strict, this hard work and this daily courage be used to ameliorate and to render more worthy of man the very life of the great majority, and that the climate and the inspiration of common life be an inspiration of generosity and a climate of heroic hope.

It is up to the supreme effort of human freedom, in the mortal struggle in which it is today engaged, to see to it that the age which we are entering is not the age of the masses, and of the shapeless multitudes nourished and brought into subjection and led to the slaughter by infamous demigods, but rather the age of the people and the man of common humanity—citizen and co-inheritor of the civilized community—cognizant of the dignity of the human person in himself, builder of a more human world directed toward an historic ideal of human brotherhood. To that effect it is necessary for the sense of the tragic in life and the sense of the great human adventure to meet and mingle, for the spirit of Europe and the spirit of America to work together in common good will. We don't believe Paradise is set for tomorrow. But the task to which we are summoned, the task we have to pursue with all the more courage and hope because at each moment it will be betrayed by human weakness, this task will have to have for objective, if we want civilization to survive, a world of free men imbued in its secular substance by a genuine and living Christianity, a world in which the inspiration of the Gospel will orient common life toward an heroic humanism.